UNIVERSAL COMMANDER

By

COLLETTE CHINYERE NLEMCHI

Gotham Books

30 N Gould St.
Ste. 20820, Sheridan, WY 82801
https://gothambooksinc.com/

Phone: 1 (307) 464-7800

Published by Gotham Books (June 15, 2023)

ISBN: 979-8-88775-298-3 (P)
ISBN: 979-8-88775-299-0 (E)

Because of the dynamic nature of the Internet, any web addresses or links contained in this book may have changed since publication and may no longer be valid.

The views expressed in this work are solely those of the author and do not necessarily reflect the views of the publisher, and the publisher hereby disclaims any responsibility for them.

TABLE OF CONTENTS

ACKNOWLEDGEMENT

First and foremost, I offer my appreciation, thanksgiving to the King of Kings and the Lord of Lords, who have given me inspiration to write. Yes, the Lord has given me the vision and there are supporters behind the Scene. My children, (Precious Kelechi Arise Nlemchi, Treasure, Onyekachi, Olanipekun Nlemchi. Genesis, Chizaram, Nlemchi, Godbolt.) They have given support for my God given Talent directly or indirectly and I pray that God will guide and protect them in all their endeavors.

POWER OF ALL POWERS

I know thou created the World.
Everything is in thy hands.
Thou commandest the day and the night.
All Powers and Glory is in your hands.

Only you have the powers to reverse things.
You know why am depending on you.
Because there is no other way.
All my trust I put in you.
For thou shall solve my problems.

Thou shall end lack in my life.
And thou shall make my cup to overflow.
And I shall praise you and
I shall stretch out my hands because thou hast blessed me.

SPEED UP MY BLESSINGS

Speed up my blessings Oh Lord.
Don't let shame be on me.
I am under your umbrella.
And thou shall miraculously surprise me.
I shall not beg for bread because,
It is only you I serve.
You are my provider for these which I need.
I know thou can do all things.
Because it is only you who is everlasting.
Thou can change things.
Only you have control over our lives.
Thou only can extend it to shame the devil.

POWERFUL GOD

Majestic, Miraculous and Powerful God.
On my knees I bow down for you.
Because thou cannot be compared with any.
The mysteries of your creation,
Makes me to wonder.
How beautiful, powerful and glorious thou art.

MANY THANKS

Almighty God, I am grateful for that which you did.
You sure did put Satan to Shame.
Remove this cloud of Darkness.
Cloud of Sorrow and mourning be removed.
And cloud of Lack be removed in Jesus Name.
Thou who reigneth forever.
How beautiful, powerful, and glorious thou art.

TEACH ME TO PROSPER OH! LORD

Almighty God, teach me to prosper and profit in Jesus
Name.
OH! Ye worshipers of Zion, Cry unto him for breakthrough.
Cry unto him for your family.
Cry unto him for your finances.
Lord gives me power for maximum protection achievement
in Jesus Name.

Every curse of profitless venture,
Upon my life, break in Jesus Name.
I refuse to labor in vain in Jesus name.

Lord let your blessings replace every curse upon my life.
Curses upon my life, break by fire in Jesus Name.
I refuse to labor in vain in Jesus Name.
Almighty God, thou shall disappoint all the,
Expectations of my enemies In Jesus Name.
Heavenly Father, make me a blessing.
And I will not lose favor in JESUS NAME.
Let my blessings receive divine speed In Jesus Name.
Any plan of the Enemies to make me suffer both at young
And old age, I say scatter by fire In Jesus Mighty Name.
Amen.

GOD OF RESTORATION

I receive mercy, prosperity, wealth and divine favor,
From the almighty God.
Heavenly, Rock of Ages, I am that I am.
The only one who lives forever.
With your power, you will blow away every antagonistic,
Satanic forces blocking my ways in your name.
Oh! God of fire and Restoration,
Return me to power and glory In Jesus Name.
Command Restoration of all my losses in your mighty
Name.
Lord of Heavens bring back all my scattered blessings in
Jesus Name.

Oh! Rock of Ages, Perfect my life and only
Your name shall be praised in Jesus Name.
Every one sick among you. Math 8. V17
He took my infirmities and healed my diseases in Jesus
Name.
Command your infirmities to be taken away.

Oh! Ye powers of darkness working against my life,
Scatter to desolation IN JESUS NAME.
Be consumed by the Holy Ghost Fire in his Mighty
name.

Power of God, Possess me and liberate me,
And my family from crises and agents of destruction,
In Jesus Name. AMEN, AMEN, AMEN.

FULFILLING MY DESTINY

I …insert your name, your children names, shall fulfil the call of God in my life, whether Satan like it or not, all In Jesus Name.
My promotion in this life shall not be taken away IN HIS MIGHTY NAME.
I…. shall not be a Waste for DEMON SPIRITS AND Satanic Agents IN JESUS NAME.
Almighty God, rearrange my life to fulfill your devine purpose of this life IN JESUS NAME.
Power of transfiguration and Resurection, manifest in my life In Jesus Name.
Oh! Lord touch my life with your finger of fire of Transfiguration in Jesus Name.
Oh! Lord surprise and bless me with signs and Wonders in Your Powerful Name.
Every labor of the Enemy upon my life, receive failure IN JESUS NAME.

THE GREATEST

The beauty you bring,
Comes in Summer, Autumn, Winter and Spring.
Your genuine love cannot be compared.
It is only in you there is perfection.
Therefore, we will try to put our trust in you.

Thou who maketh Heaven and Earth,
And everything you created adores thee.
The Earth moves around the globe.
And all Heavenly bodies Adoreth thee.
How wonderful, powerful and Glorious thou art.
If only we can trust thee and have faith,
We shall eat bountifully the fruit of the land.
Oh! Mysterious one thou art indeed the greatest.

THOU ART POWERFUL

How wonderful art thou who created Heaven and Earth.
You made the Heaven and Earth, thou art wonderful.
You created human beings, thou art wonderful.
You spread the land on waters thou art wonderful.

You Slaughtered famous kings.
Your love is everlasting.
You led the people of isreal into the wilderness.
Your love is everlasting.
You made Day and Night.
Your love is Everlasting.

The Sun, Moon, and the Stars adore thee.
You are the greatest.
You made the Rivers, Oceans and Sea.
Thou art the greatest.
You healeth the sick, lame and Dump.
Thou art Miraculous.

EVERLASTING FATHER

I will honor thee and lift your name high.
Lift your name high, above the sky.
Heaven knows how I adore thee.
Because none and none is like thee in this world we live.

Oh! Perfection, thou art the greatest.
Nothing can be compared with thee.
No creature created is greater than thee.
You are the greatest one indeed.

You gave me the brain to think and reason.
Knowing the Power beyond and above.
This wonderful Power made the Universe
And all the inhabitants that dwells in it.

Thou are the greatest Commander.
Mankind fool around like Zombies.
As they take care of their business and Marketing.
And when the time comes.
They disappear from the surface of the Earth.
Only You Mighty One That Lives forever.

POWERFUL ONE

Thou who created Heaven and Earth.
You formed me from my Mother's Womb.
You said let there be light and there was light.
Thou only have all the powers in this World.

Where is my Destiny Oh! Mighty one.
Speed up my Destiny.
I am hasting to do thy will.
You have all the powers to crush,
Anybody holding my Destiny.

I come against every attack against my breakthrough.
Power of Powers, thou shall stop all hindering spirits.
All Demonic forces, working against my devine calling,
You must bow in Jesus Name.

BOOK OF WISDOM

I am able to read the Bible.
Because I am able.
Scripture inspired and given by the Lord.
And the Scribes Who Wrote the Bible.
All heard the Word.
The Book is the Best Book to Read.
From The Book You Know the Wisdom.
My Ancestors Read The Book of Knowledge.
Passing it down to their Descendants.

CANCEL, SEAL AND RECLAIM

1. I Cancel Injustice in my life and I seal it In Jesus Name.
2. I Cancel bad luck in my life and I seal it IN JESUS NAME.
3. I Cancel procrastination in my life and I seal it. IJN.
4. I Cancel lack of favor in my life and I seal it in Jesus Name.
5. I Cancel the Power of My Enemies Over My Finances and I Seal It in JESUS NAME.
6. I Reclaim Garment of Favor IN JESUS NAME.
7. I Cancel My Enemies and Their Evil Plans IN JESUS NAME.
8. I Cancel Licking Pocket IN JESUS NAME.
9. I Claim Good Luck in Jesus Name.
10. I Cancel Premature Death in My Life and The Life of My Children IN JESUS NAME.
11. I Claim fulfilment of Destiny on my Life and My Children's Life IN JESUS NAME.

I AM THE WAY

I am the Way You Said My Lord.
I am the Way You Said My King.
There are many Ways in This World.
The Ways of The Lord Is Glorious.

Your Way Oh! Mighty One is The Best.
When I was Wondering Around the Desert,
I did not know Which Way to Follow.
You Gave Me Directions and Lead Me Through.

Even In My Sadness and Agony, I followed Your Ways.
Even When Am Helpless and Hopeless, I Followed Your
Ways.
Your Foot Prints Oh! Lord I will Follow.
Your Path My Father, I will Follow.
When Lucifer comes With Lying Tongue,
Oh! Jesus, I followed Your Ways.

My Forefathers, those you anointed,
They all followed Your Ways.
My Ancestors, Those Who You Promised,
They all followed your ways.
They were obedient till the end.
Lord, your promises we will rekindle.
Lord, your directions I will follow.

<u>PRAYER FOR THE SICK</u>

Thou art the Greatest Physician on Earth.
Thou Miraculously curest with no medicine or Acupuncture.
Thy Holy Hand Touches Me and I am Healed.
Father of all Fathers help the Sick and the Helpless.
Touch Us with Thy Holy Hands and We Shall Recover.

Jesus, let us recount all your Miracles.
You Healed the leper with no Medicine.
The Centurion Servant You Healed.
The Woman with an issue of Blood, You Healed.
You Healed the lame and the Blind.
And thou taketh away all generational Curses.
Oh! Heavenly Father, thou healeth Cancer, Diabetes,
and all kinds of Sicknesses and diseases.
Thank you Lord for Healing me.
Master, with your stripes I am healed IN JESUS NAME.

PRAYER FOR FORGIVENESS

Lord, who am I to bear grudges against my fellow Human
Being?
And I ask who am I to Judge?
Oh! King of Kings who judges and sees Everything,
I am asking you not to hold these grudges against my foes.
Lord anoint my spirit and do not let me hold grudges
against anybody.
Who am I to hold grudges against anybody?
As you have forgiven me my sins so shall I forgive any who
sin against me.
I know with openness of heart and good spirit,
Your will shall be done in my life.
The openness of heart makes us to find favor with the
Angels and the Lord.

SUPERNATURAL FAITH

Lord, I thank you for being our God who is greater than Everything.
The world bows down for you, Oh! Omnipotent and Powerful God.
With supernatural faith, I am healed from my infirmities.
With your power, all Principalities, Spiritual Wickedness, Standing against my break through must be crushed IN JESUS NAME.
All Satanic Barriers on my Pathway must be Removed IN JESUS NAME.
All Witches and Wizards Working Against My Life Must Be Destroyed.
Forces of Darkness in this House, causing me and my children bad Luck
Be ye removed by the Power of the Almighty God.

MOUNTAIN MOVER

Oh! Ye mountains in my life, be ye removed IN JESUS NAME.
Mountain of Poverty, Run away IN JESUS NAME.
Mountain of Bad Spirit, I command you to get out IN JESUS NAME.
Mountain of Bad Relationship upon me and my Children, I say Catch fire IJN.
Any Fake Vodoo Church, Shrine or Anywhere they have my name and my Children Name, I say Catch Fire IN JESUS NAME.
I Cancel any Decree by Satanic Forces and their Agents that I will not make it, I say Catch Fire in Jesus Name Amen.
Oh! Ye My Footsteps' thou shall be divinely directed IN JESUS NAME.
Oh! Ye Mountains of Sicknesses and Diseases in my Body, I Command You to Disappear by Fire in Jesus Name.
I decree that all my blessings for me and my Children shall be Permanent IN JESUS NAME.
Oh! YeStealers of my Heavenly Blessings, I Command You to Vomit Every Stolen Blessings and be Consumed by The Holy Ghost Fire IN JESUS NAME.

<u>YOUR KINGDOM REIGNETH FOREVER</u>

Thy Kingdom will reign forever.
Thou who created Heaven and Earth.
You created all the Rivers and the Oceans.
Your Ways Oh! Lord is beyond Human Understanding.
It is only you who gives and takes.
All powers in this world belongs to you.
You made the Heavens and the Earth.
The Seas, Rivers, and the Oceans,
Are all your Creation.
The beautiful, Roses and the Lillies in the garden are all yours.
Move thou my Mountains and thou destroyeth all obstacles on my Pathway in JESUS NAME.

I ADORETH THEE

Lord, give me love where there is hatred.
Perfection where there is imperfection.
Upliftment where there is let down.
Crush all upstacles on my pathway.
The mountains shall sing while the rivers rejoice.
Many have come and gone.
We ask where are they going?
This mysterious life goes on and on.
Are you not a foolnot to believe in higher and extraordinary
power?
Oh! Mysterious one, the signs you show us liveth forever.
In our memory it shall be made permanent.
Devine workers are happy for their call.
They do their work diligently without complain.
Oh! Perfection, I adoreth thee.
Youerected the pillar that holdeth this Universe.
Thou art Omnipotent and Powerful.
Your wonders cannot be explained.
I thank you for all your blessings.
You made the big and small.
And the whole universe depends on you.

THE WIND OF FAITH

The mysterious and the invisible wind.
You passed me by with a healing touch.
You left a fragrance that smelleth like Heaven.
You restored my broken bone.
From Head to My Toes Thou Healeth me.

You made a way for me in the Wilderness.
At the Pool of Waters, Thou Washet Me.
You gave me Water to Drink and said,
You will never Thirst Again.
Master, thanks for Your Kindness.
You made me to see that which seems Impossible.
You Clothed me, Elevated Me and Made Me to Sit with
Angels.
Thou art the Purest of All Gods.

THE GREATEST ONE

The Highest One, thou who made the Heavens and the Earth.
Come Down to my Rescue. Heal thou me from these infirmities that is on me.
Cleans me and make me whither than snow.
Renew the Broken Bones in My Body.
Thou who is the Greatest Commander.
Thou who Created both the Big and Small.
With your Power, all evil against my life shall be destroyed.
Are you not the power that restoreth the innocent from the Wicked?
Mighty One I shall not be put to shame While Serving You.

Send down your Powerful Angels around me, and they shall be my guide.
I will serve you throughout the days of my life.
The Pillar that Holdeth this World.
Who is Greater than You?.None.
I am Honored and glad to be among the Chosen.
Whatever you want me to do, I shall Obey Thee.
Thou Who Reignet for ever and ever.

ATTACKING MY SPIRITUAL ATTACKERS

Any forces attacking my spiritual life must be destroyed IN JESUS NAME.
All Witches and Wizards Trying so Hard to Stop My Destiny Must Receive Fire from Heaven IN JESUS NAME.
OH! Mighty One, I am Healed with your Stripes. AMEN

NONE LIKE THEE

Thou art the Lord our God, None like thee.
Thou who made Day and Night, None Like Thee.
Thou who Healeth the Sick, None Like Thee.
Thou Who Slauthered Demons, None like Thee.
Thou Who Slauthered Famous Kings, None like Thee.
Thou who made the Isrealites Cross the Red Sea, None
LIke Thee.
Thou who change things Miraculously, none like thee.
Thou who is a Mountain Mover, None like you.
Thou who buttered my bread, none like you.
Thou who gave me and my Children longer Years, None
like Thee.
Thou who heal all my sicknesses and diseases, none like
thee.
Thou whose handwork cannot be compared, none like thee.
Thou who giveth and taketh, none like thee.
Thou who gave me blessings, none like thee.
Thou who liveth forever, none like thee.

THE GOD OF IMPOSSIBILITY

The God impossibility. I command all impossibilities in my life possible.
The God that create and restores, Create and Restore a new Thing in My Life.
The God that opens the Gates of Heaven. Open up the gates of Heaven and Pour out blessings in your Holy Name.
The God that heals the sick, Heal my sickness and Diseases in your mighty name.
The God that Protect every movement I take, please protect my movements.
The God of Fire, Fire all my challenges in your POWERFUL NAME.
The God that changes people in a twinkle of an eye. Change my life.
The God of many Rivers. The God that heals the sick. Heal my infirmities
OH! Loving and kind God…one who is good beyond measures, Master be good to me.
The God who protects his saints. Protect me and my Children INJESUS NAME..
ALMIGHTY ONE, I SALUTE YOU OH! KING OF KINGS.

THE HEALING GOD

The powerful and Invisible Wind.
Thou Passeth me by, with a healing Touch.
Thou leaveth a fragrance that smelleth like Heaven.
Thou Restoreth my broken bones.
From head to my toes, thou cleansed me.
You made a way for me in the Wilderness.
At the pool of Waters, you washed me.
You gave me water to drink and said "thou shall not thirst
again".
You made me to see that which seems to be impossible.
Thanks, and many thanks for your kindness.
You gave me wealth, clothed me and made me to sit with
Angels.
You are the Purest of all gods. THOU ART GOD INDEED.
You gave me CROWN which I will never throw away.
It is a sacred and a HOLY CROWN.
Heaven bare me witness, I will never forget your kindness.
You healed me, protected me and made me strong.

PROTECTION

Heavenly Father, I am counting on you for protection.
Ancient of days, I am asking for your blessings.
Whatever I do, I ask for your protection.
Wherever I go, I ask for your protection.
The Children you gave me I ask for their protection.
All my Assets, I ask for protection IN JESUS NAME.

THE GOD OF PERFECTION

The God of Perfection.
Thou created this world of Perfection and Confusion.
Some have found Satisfaction.
With their life of corruption.
Thou givet us choices.
To choose in this world of Tribulations.
The Chosen ones are doing meditations to serve and
Honor the God of Perfection.

TRUST IN YOU

I put my Trust in You.
When facing Problems and Trials.
I Put my trust in you.
In this World of Imperfection.
Even if I have tried and failed.
I put my trust in You.
The Creator of this World.
Thou shall perfect my Journey.
Thou shall surprise me when least expected.
And I shall thank thee all my life.
I shall be glad and merry.
Because thou savest me.
And lifted me up from the pit.
Oh! Mighty and perfect one.
I shall serve thee all my life.

THE CROSS OF LIFE

Thou woke me up in the middle of the night.
Giving me courage to move on.
Thou art the greatest, I shall not fear.
Thou lovet me as your child.
And I will carry the Cross of life.

I know thou shall send Angels to me.
From all four corners of the world.
They shall come.
They shall deliver the message.
The message of Wealth and good Will.
They will give to me.
I shall not serve thee in vain.
Because thou reward those that serve thee.
Thou are perfect and will not let me fail.
Mighty one, thou art good, powerful and great.
And the world is all about you.

A WAY IN THE WILDERNESS

All my hindrances shall be crushed.
They will enter into the pits of hail.
And Satan will be their friend.
Perfection did not approve their wickedness.
For trying to destroy the child of Destiny.

Oh! Perfection, I adore and honor thee.
I shall bow down for thee.
And I shall worship thee.
The one that changes things.
Thou will wipe away my imperfection.
And I shall serve thee forever.
Thou maket a way for me in the wilderness.
When am lonely and wondering.
Looking for answers here and there.
And thou comet to my rescue.
And saveth me from danger.
Thou are powerful and Mighty one.
And thou art the greatest one indeed.

<u>I SHALL NOT WANT</u>

Thou who made Heaven and Earth.
I shall not fear or be Afraid.
Even if acquaintances turn their back on me.
I will always put my trust in you.
Because thou shall mend my broken Heart.
There is none that serve you to be put to shame.
Your Kingdom People thou shall protect.
And thou shall fill my Emptiness with your greatness.
Thou art the greatest one indeed.
Miracle one you are.
You turned my mourning into joy.
You lifted me up from the pit.
All opstacles you have crushed.
Because thou loveth me forever.
And I shall not want.

GIVING THANKS

Creator of this World, Omnipotent Daddy, I thank you.
For the air I breath, and life you gave me, I thank you.
For my answered prayers, Lord, I thank you.
Glorious Father, I thank you for making a way for me.
And the Children you gave me, I thank you.

The greatest one, you made my impossibilities become possible.
This week, thou will send my prosperity Angels and no blessings shall pass me by.
I will grab all my blessings on my pathway.
And will not let go unless they bless me.
Thou giveth me the power to grab my blessings.
Thank you for, forgiving my Sins and Blessing me.

THE DIVINE WIND

Oh! Wind of Change, locate me.
Forget not my stumbling blocks.
As I move and look, I sense you in me.
For seven times you blow through my ways.
The damsels shall bare me witness.

Even in the midst of storm, you did remember me.
From South Pole You Blow Through the Trees.
The flowers Sing as you pass by.
You nourish them and left a memory.
And they will never forget your ways.

The birds have found favor in you.
As they humbly sing and wait for you.
For the restoration you promised.
A time will come when they will see you.
Their eyes are waiting for the promise.

How happy and innocent they look.
Simple life they live.
Here comes the Kingdom they hope for.
While waiting for mankind Restoration.

MYSTERIOUS EYES

Let us join hands together for love.
Many have seen the light, but still in dark.
It comes in disguise for us to guess.
But the light was only seen by the dove.
He saw the light because his eyes are wide awake.

The Whole Cosmos are in Slumber.
Their eyes are open but they cannot see.
It is only the flashiness they can remember.
Shame, Shame, the Banished Children of Eve.
For the Light has come and passed you by.

MAN'S IGNORANCE

The whole Cosmos are in shamble.
Mankind move around in a field of many dreams.
Man does not know the cause of things.
They pursue vain and foolish ambitions.
Science is curious but does not have all the answers.

Mankind did invent artificial lights, Robots and Computers.
But Man's ignorance and stupidity,
Knoweth not the mysteriesof this life.
However, Mankind should be aware that all belongs to him.
WHO GIVETH US THE LIGHT.

THE BIGNESS OF OUR GOD

Worried about your bills, your problems,
Isaiah 41:10." Fear thou not, for I am with thee, be
Not dismayed for I am thy God: I will strengthen thee
Yea, I will help thee; yea, I will uphold thee with
The right hand of Righteousness."

God is richer than our depths (Phillipians 4:19) God is
Better than our Faith. (Mathew 17:20)
God is stronger than our Enemies. (Psalms 18:3)
Have the Armor of God to Protect You From all Your Foes.
(Ephesians 6:11-18)

PRAYER FOR HEALING

This prayer is for overall healing of the body. All the organs of the body shall be prayed for. The God we serve is a Powerful and Mighty God.
He heals with no medicine or acupuncture.
The GREATEST PHYSICIAN HE IS.
In this prayer points, we shall attack all organs of the body that is afflicted with all kinds of infirmities and afflictions.
Folks, thou shall command your Healing.
MY HEAD: Oh! Lord heal me from all afflictions and the infirmities associated with the brain IN JESUS NAME. MY EYES: Oh! Lord heal me from all afflictions and infirmities of the eyes IN JESUS NAME.
MY FACE: Oh! Lord, heal me from all the afflictions and infirmities of the face IN JESUS NAME.
MY MOUTH: Oh! Lord heal me from all the afflictions and infirmities of the mouth IN JESUS NAME.
MY NECK: Oh! Lord, heal me from all the afflictions and infirmities of the neck IN JESUS NAME.
MY HEART: Oh! Lord heal me from all the afflictions and Infirmities of the Heart IN JESUS NAME.
MY STOMACH: Oh! Lord, heal me from all the afflictions and infirmities of the Stomach IN JESUS NAME.
MY LEGS AND HANDS. Oh! Lord, heal me from all the afflictions and infirmities of the Legs and Hands IN JESUS NAME.

OMNIPOTENT DADDY

Thou art the omnipotent Daddy.
You the God of Transformation.
Thou sitteth at the sit of Perfection.
Forgiveth all my sins of Omission.
Unto your Kingdom I receive Admission.

Eternal life thou hath given me.
Joy unspeakable both on Earth and in Heaven.
And I shall dwell among the Hollies.
24hrs we shall praise thee.
Because thou art the greatest one.
Who holdeth the pillars of this World.

Wonderful and Powerful One.
All glory and Honor goes to you.
Mankind will decrease and thou shall increase. Thou
who reigneth forever.
I bow down for you.

UNIVERSAL COMMANDER

Words cannot explain.
Neither can eye tell.
What the Lord will do for those who serve him.

The rain drops will testify.
The wind shall prophecy.
The Oceans will rejoice.
For the Wonders you do.

How Wonderful and Powerful you are.
You pick up the rejected.
The abused and lonely.
And thou did put at High Places.

Cherubis are happy for you.
Holy Seraphins will rejoice.
For that which you did.
The Compassionate and Holy One.
Guide us as we dance to your Tone.

ALL POWERS BELONG TO YOU

Thou who Commandest the Heaven and Earth.
Thou who sees the living and the Dead.
Thou who created Mankind.
Thou Whose Mercy Cannot be Compared.
Thou art Wonderful.

You hold all the Powers in this World.
All Creatures are Bowing Down for You.
Thou who forgives and Restores.
Restoration Daddy, I call Thee.

Restore that which is missing in my life.
And bring to perfection that which is not Perfect.
Thou art the Beginning and Thou art the End.

SPIRITUAL LAWS OF PROSPERITY

This talks about Prosperity which is Universal and Anyone who abides by it will reap a reward. Father, I thank you for this Knowledge and let it be good for my readers.

Luke 12:32. "Fear not, little flock; for it is the will of your Father's good pleasure to give you the Kingdom.
1 Corinthians: 3:16. "Know ye not that ye are the Temple of God, and the Spirit of God dwelleth in you.
John 10:34."ye are Gods" Means you are a Co-Creator of the World you live in.
Mark 9:23. "If thou canst believe all things are possible to him that believeth.
Philippians 4:19: But my God shall supply all your needs according to his riches in Christ Jesus.
1. Samuel 2:7. Thou maketh poor and Rich.
Nehemiah 2:20: The God of Heavens He will Prosper Us.
Deuteronomy 8: 18: But thou shall remember the Lord thy God, for it is he that giveth thee power to make wealth.
1 Timothy 6: 17. "God, who giveth us richly all things to enjoy.
Oh! Divine substance please prosper.

MASTER DESIGNER

Master thou art the Author of Redemption.
Who Designet Creation.
Thou Speaketh Revelation.
To avoid Mankind Confusion.
History will remember you as Sovereignty.
In this land of Persecution.
I salute you Oh! Devine Master.
Who livet Forever and Ever.

CHAMPION OF THE UNIVERSE

Blessed is those who serve and worship thee.
Thy Kingdom they shall inherit.
Thou direct their Footsteps.
As they Gloriously lift thy Holy Name High.
Magnificent and Powerful One.
All Glory and Adoration unto thy Holy Name.
Oh! Champion of The Universe.

INVOKING THE ANGELS

Brethren, Our Heavenly Father have Angels who are also messengers. They go around the Globe doing the work of the Lord. They come in different forms, shapes and Sizes. The Holy Scripture has told us to be good to strangers because you do not know when you will entertain Angels Unawares. Sometimes, you see a crooked person, you laugh and criticize not knowing that the person is a messenger from God. In this Message, we should ask God to give us insight, Compassionate heart to embrace Angels. Oh! Lord, is all by your power. Help me to know and embrace my Angels when they come. Say these Prayer Points and when your Angels come, they will not pass you by.Remember, your Angels may not have wings, God can use people to minister to you. Oh! Powerful Angels of God, Angels of Power, Angels of good Health, Angels of Prosperity, Angels of Protection, Come and Visit Me IN JESUS NAME. (7 Times).

THE CHOSEN ONE

When the days are rough you make a way.
The breakthrough you do no Man can Object.
The doors you open, no man can shut.
You protect my movement and my part you Direct.
The birds are eating the crumbs, soon they fly away.

The hope of Mankind is in You.
Mankind cannot defile what you have blessed.
The evil plans they do goes back to them.
Mankind has no power but to watch your wrath.

Heaven, I know your promise must come to pass.
The Mockers, bystanders, hindrances will just watch.
As you save me from the storm.

Day and Night I magnify and praise your Name.
You should not forsake me or abandon me.
For those who seek you, should be rewarded.
So that we cannot labor in vain.
Thanks, Heaven, for making me to be one of the chosen
ones.

GOD OF RESTORATION

Holy Master, Restore, Repair and Revive.
Bring back to life, what is stolen.
Bring back to life what is cursed.
Your divine restoration stoppeth the storm.
Master, bring back hope where hope is lost.

In thee I trust and all my hopes are on you.
Mankind will Propose and you will Dispose.
The World is in thy Hands.
You are the Compassionate one.
The only and divine hope of mankind.

GLORIFY HIS NAME

All honor and glory belongs to you.
Mankind will decrease and you will increase.
The hope of mankind is in you.
Because all Powers Belong to You.

Master, it is only by thy power.
Not the power of Mankind.
Changest not your mind on me.
Give me Restoration.
And do not leave me.

Help us to fight this battle of life.
For all our hopes are in thee.
The power you have cannot be compared.
You are the greatest and the most powerful,
Than anything under the surface of the Sun.

MASTER AVENGE WICKED SPIRITS

Master it is only you who is powerful.
Will you allow these wicked spirits to prevail.
Injustice and wickedness have filled the Earth.
Master avenges these spirits who are standing on the way.
Holy Master you know my plight.
Thou knowet everything that is hidden under the sun.

Master of all Masters Avenge and Avenge.
Holy and powerful Angels.
Go and Avenge for this battle is God's.
Avenge against wickedness and evil.
Master, I say Avenge and Avenge.

ARISE MY DESTINY

Holy Master, glorious one, thou shall reign forever.
My whole duty is to praise and glorify you.
Please Master, restore, repair and bring to life.
That which is cast away by demon spirits.
Bring to life that which is forsaken.

I look at your hand work, and I call you Master Designer.
I am beautiful and wonderfully made.
This destiny, which you trusted upon me.
Cannot be delayed by Satanic forces anymore.
Release, Master, the Power of my Destiny.
Which you have already designed.

How wonderful and powerful you are.
Thou art the hope of Mankind.
The Supreme of all Supremes.
The most magnificent one.
I adore you, and I glorify thy greatness.
All these I plead in the mighty name of Jesus.

HEAVEN HELP ME

When I am going through the storms of life,
I cry Oh! Heaven help me.
In the midst of confusion and persecution,
I cry OH! Heaven help me.
Facing condemnation,
I cry OH! Heaven help me.
He had Compassion for me.
Forgave all my Sins.
And lifted me up from the Pits of Life.
All Honor, Power, and Glory be unto Thee.

CHILD OF PROMISE REGAINS

As I look through the glass,
I see the Rainbow above the Sky.
I shouted and appreciated the colors,
Because the Heavens promise is coming.

Though, the expected time seem to be far.
But the wonders of his actions you cannot explain.
It will happen like a dream.
And before you know it, I see myself regain.

Child of Destiny, you will regain the Kingdom you lost.
And the Angels will abide with you.
They will raise you up, wipe off your dust.
Because you are a child of Promise.

KINGDOM PEOPLE

They will be shaken, cursed and rejected.
But the kingdom belongs to them.
They will be forsaken.
Yet the Kingdom belongs to them.
Their nature is to live a righteous and make peace.
Demon spirits does not like anything divine.
But the Kingdom belongs to them.
As they sweep the dust for the Master.

Master shall reward their faithfulness.
And their movement and labor of love,
Shall not go in vain.
The compassionate one will carry them on his hands.
And at last the Victory belongs to them.
Because they are the Kingdom People.

They have gone astray with wickedness.
They do not know who holds the pillars of this world.
Their wickedness has filled the Earth.
And inside the Holy Places they defile the Temple.

They did not respect his Holiness.
They do all kinds of Evil upon Evil.
Master will avenge their wickedness.
As he said "Mess not with my anointed ones.
And to my Prophets, do no harm.
These decree he passed must come to pass.
Wickedness of mankind has filled the Earth.

MIGHTY WARRIOR IN BATTLE

Here comes the Rock who knows Everything.
At his throne We bow Down.
He is Honored above all Gods.
His Kingdom Reignet Forever.
The order of the Universe belongs to him.
He reverses things for the Righteous and faithful ones.
Though Compassionate and Kind,
He is the Mighty Warrior in Battle.

BANISHMENT OF EVIL

You evil forces that are threatening me must be destroyed. All my losses, thou shall transform to my gain IN JESUS NAME.
I shall claim love, hope, happiness and prosperity IN JESUS NAME.
My lack shall be transformed to Riches, Abundance and gain.

Ye evil forces that have caused me setbacks, hindrance, and threatened to destroy my existence, thou must be Destroyed, Demolished, Austracized, Isolated, Judged , Neutralized, and Sentenced by the Almighty God Forever.

Oh! Ye my luck, I Command thee to resurrect, Miraculously Jump Out, Powerfully, and Dramatically improve IN JESUS NAME. I shall be treated with Honor and Respect. IN JESUS NAME
Oh! Ye good news, Wealth, and Miracles, thou shall locate me IN JESUS NAME.

All the Attacks from the Enemies, Known and Unknown, Oh! Mysterious Power, they shall not Succeed, and all diverted luck, Stolen Blessings, Thou Shall Come Back To me and I Shall Possess My Possession IN HIS MIGHTY NAME. AMEN.

THE NAMES OF GOD

Elohim-God (Genesis 1:1) The strong Creator.
Jehovah-LORD (Genesis 2:4) Self Existing One.
Adonai-LORD/Master (Genesis 15:2) Headship name.
Jehovah El Elohim (Joshua 22:22) The Lord God of Gods.
Jehovah Elohim (Gen2:4, 3:9-13,21) The LORD GOD
Jehovah Elohe Abothekem (Joshua 18:3) THE LORD GOD
YOUR FATHER
EL SHADDAH- All-Sufficient, all Bountiful, Almighty God,
thou taketh care of me.
JEHOVAH-JIREH-My provider! You are the one who
makes provision for me. Thou who sees all my needs and
provided redemption for my soul.
JEHOVAH-RAPHA-My healer! You are the one who heals
my spirit, soul and body.
JEHOVAH- SHALOM-My peace! You have my heart and
my soul and you gave me divine rest! I amwholly reconciled
to you.
JEHOVAH-TSIDKENU- My righteousness! You are the only
one that make it right for me.
JEHOVAH-SHAMMAH-My ever-present God! You are
always there. You never leave me or forsake me. Your
fullness and Glory dwells in me.
JEHOVAH-RO'I- My Shepherd! You guide me with love
and correct me with kindness! Thou art my Companion,
Guardian, and Savior.

<u>MEMORY VERSES FROM THE BIBLE</u>

John 3:16---For God so loved the world that he gave his only
Son that whoever believes in him should not perish but have Eternal Life.
Phillippians 4:6----Do not be anxious for anything, but in everything, by prayers and petition, with thanks giving, present your case to God.
Romans 12:2: and do not be conformed to the world, but be transformed by the renewing of your mind,that you may prove what is that good and acceptable and perfect will of God
GALATIANS 2:20: I have been crucified with Christ and am no longer live, but Christ lives in me. The life I live in the body, I live by faith in the son God, who loved me and gave himself for me.
ROMANS 6:23. For the wages of sin is death, but thegift of God is eternal life in Christ Jesus our Lord.
ROMANS 12:1. Therefore, I urge you, brother, in view of God's mercy, to offer your bodies as a living sacrifice, holy and acceptable to God, which is Your Spiritual worship.
EPHESIANS 2:8. For by grace you have been saved through faith, and that not of yourselves, it is the gift of God.
And the peace of God, which surpasses all comprehension, will guard your hearts and your minds in Christ Jesus.
Romans 8:28. And we know that in all things God works for the good of those who love him, who have been called according to his will.
Psalm 1:1. Blessed is the man who does not walk in the counsel of the Wicked or Sit in the Seat of Mockers.

SCRIPTURES FROM THE BIBLE AND THE

BOOK OF MORMON

John 3:16 (God of Love)
Acts 7:55-56 (Son at the right hand of the Father)
D&C 88:41-44 (Attributes of God)
Psalm 24:1 (The Earth is the Lord's)
Moses 1:30-39 (Creation)
Alma 7:20 (God Cannot do wrong)
Joseph Smith ----History 1:17 (Father and Son are
Separate Beings)
Alma 5:40 (good comes from God)
John 14:6-9 (Son and Father are alike)
Mormon 9:15-20 (God of Miracles)
John 14:6-9 (Son and Father are alike)
Mormon 9:15-20(God of Miracles)
John 3:16 (God of love)
Job 38:4-7 (Premortal life implied)
Abraham 3:22-28 (Vision of premortal life)
Jeremiah 1:5 (Vision of premortal life)
D &C 29:31-38 Vision of premortal life)
Moses 3:4-7 (Spiritual and Temporal Creations)
MOSES 4: 1-4; Abraham 3:22-28 (Savior Chosen in
Premortality)
D & C 76:25-29 (War in Heaven)
REVELATION 12:7-9, 11 (The Lord's Followers in the War
in Heaven defeated Satan by the Blood of Jesus and by the
word of Testimony
ISAIAH 14:12-15 Lucifer cast out and defeated)

HEALING PRAYERS

Jesus is a great physcician. He healed all manner of sicknesses and diseases during his earthly ministry on Earth. His Miracles and healing Power continues till this day. Study these verses and thou shall be healed.
Psalm 41:3. "The Lord will strengthen him on his bed of illness; You will Sustain him on his sickbed."
Psalm 42:11. Why are you down, O my soul? And why are you disquieted within me? Hope in God; for I shall yet praise Him, The help of my countenance and my God."
Everyone who has this hope in him purifies himself, just as he is pure. (1 John3:33)
"But I will restore you to health and heal your wounds, declares the Lord. (Jeremiah 30:17)
JAMES 1:6,7 "But let him ask in faith without doubting, for he who doubts is like a wave of the sea driven and tossed by the Wind. For let not that man suppose that he will receive anything from the Lord; he is a double minded man,unstable in all his ways." .
1 John 5: 14,15." If we ask anything according to his will, he hears us and if we knows that he hears us in whatever we ask, we know that we have the requests which we have asked him."

THY NAME MUST BE GLORIFIED

Oh! Highest heaven, thy name must be glorified
One who is at the highest throne, thy name must be
glorified
Father of all fathers, thy name must be glorified
Omnipotent Daddy, thy name must be glorified
One who made Heaven and Earth, thy name must be
glorified
The power that holdeth this world, thy name must be
glorified
Ancient of days, thy name must be glorified
Power, that controls all powers, thy name must be glorified.

Invisible Spirit, thy name must be glorified in

JESUS NAME WHETHER SATAN LIKE IT OR NOT, THY NAME MUST BE GLORIFIED IN JESUS NAME AMEN.

Well in Twelve

Alycea K. Shirley
Well in Twelve

Copyright © 2025 by Alycea K. Shirley

ISBN 979-8-89691-521-8